Learn to Read with EP

First Edition

Welcome to Easy Peasy All-in-One Homeschool's Learn to Read course. This course will take your child from knowing the alphabet to being a proficient reader, able to read full-length novels.

The course is in three parts: sight words, practice and phonics.

CONTENTS

ACKNOWLEDGEMENTS

Thank you to Michelle Kierznowski for her cover art work.

I have borrowed the structure of the phonics section from *Phonics Pathways*, in going from two sounds to three sounds, to ending blends, to long vowel sounds, etc. I used that book with my first kids to teach them phonics. I have created this phonics section with my own examples, but I wanted to acknowledge where I came up with the structure I use.

Part 1: <u>The McGuffey Eclectic Primer</u>

Students begin by learning sight words. Sight reading will help your child learn to read quickly and fluently. You are reading this by sight right now. Being able to read by sight is the goal of learning to read. Phonics is the tool we use when we come across a word we don't know by sight. The students will learn to use phonics later in this course.

How to use part 1:

Each day the student will learn the sight words. Show your child each word individually, covering up the others with a piece of paper or large index card. Read the word to your child and then have the child read the word to you. Then you can show a word and ask your child if he knows it. If not, that's fine. Say it to him and have him read it to you.

Do this three times a day, maybe breakfast, lunch and dinner so it's anchored in your day and not forgotten.

After the final practice, hopefully your child knows the words, even if he needs a little prompting, such as, "What letter does it start with? What sound does that make?" Now's the time to read the lesson. Have the child read the lesson to you.

You can help your child use the pictures for clues to help him read. You can also ask questions like described above, "What letter does it start with?" "What sound does that make?" You can also point out things like the "at" in mat and ask what that says. Then ask what does the word start with and what do they sound like put together.

If your child can't remember the words and just isn't getting it, I suggest putting it aside for six months, focus on letters and their phonetic sounds and then try again.

On days when there is a review reading, there are no words to practice. You might want to split those readings up during your reading times during the day since they are longer. It's also a good idea to pick a sentence from it to have your child read again, fast. This can help in practicing fluency and will develop confidence and comprehension.

McGUFFEY'S®

ECLECTIC PRIMER.

THE ALPHABET.

A B C D

E F G H

I J K L

M N O P

Q R S T

U V W X

 Y Z

THE ALPHABET.

a b c d

e f g h

i j k l

m n o p

q r s t

u v w x

 y z

3

a

cat

rat

and

a   ănd   căt   răt

ă   e   d   n   r   t

a rat   a cat

A cat   A rat

A cat and a rat.

A rat and a cat.

at

the

ran

has

Ann

LESSON II.

ăt   the   răn   hăș

Ănn

h   th   ș

The cat   the rat

The cat has a rat.

The rat ran at Ann.

Ann has a cat.

The cat ran at the rat.

Nat

hat

fan

can

LESSON III.

Năt   hăt   făn   căn

f

a fan   a hat

Ann and Nat.

Ann has a fan.

Nat has a hat.

Ann can fan Nat.

man

cap

lad

sat

LESSON IV.

măn   căp

lăd   săt

l   m   p   s

a cap   the lad

A man and a lad.

The man sat; the lad ran.

The man has a hat.

The lad has a cap.

LESSON V.-REVIEW.

The cat and the rat ran.

Ann sat, and Nat ran.

A rat ran at Nat.

Can Ann fan the lad?

The man and the lad.

The man has a cap.

The lad has a fan.

Has Ann a hat?

Ann has a hat and a fan.

dog

Rab

fat

Nat's

LESSON VI.

dŏḡ   Răb

făt   Năt's

ŏ   b   ḡ

Nat's cap   a fat dog

Has the lad a dog?

The lad has a fat dog.

The dog has Nat's cap.

Nat and Rab ran.

Rab ran at a cat.

14

see

sees

frog

on

log

LESSON VII.

sēe   sēes̸   frŏḡ

ŏn   lŏḡ

ē

a log   the frog

See the frog on a log.

Rab sees the frog.

Can the frog see Rab?

The frog can see the dog.

Rab ran at the frog.

it   is

stand

Ann's

lamp

mat

LESSON VIII.

ĭt	stănd	Ann'ş
ĭş	lămp	măt
	ĭ	

a mat   the stand

See the lamp! It is on a mat.

The mat is on the stand.

The lamp is Nat's, and the mat is Ann's.

18

Lesson 9

Tom

nag

not

he

*more words on the next page

him

his

catch

LESSON IX.

Tŏm	năḡ	nŏt
hĭm	cătch	hē
hĭṣ		ch

See the nag! It is Tom's nag.

Can Tom catch his nag?

He can not catch him.

The dog ran at the nag, and the nag ran.

Tom's nag is fat; his dog is not fat.

Nat is on Tom's nag.

Nat's dog, Rab, can not catch the rat.

See the frog on the log.

A lad sees the frog.

The lad can not catch it.

A cat is on the mat; the cat sees a rat.

Ann's fan is on the stand.

The man has a lamp.

A dog ran at the man.

Ann sat on a log.

nest

this

eggs

she

*more words on the next page

in

get

box

hen

LESSON XI

nĕst   thĭs   ĕḡḡs   shē

ĭn   ḡĕt

bŏx   hĕn

ĕ   x   sh

the box   a nest

This is a fat hen.

The hen has a nest in the box.

She has eggs in the nest.

A cat sees the nest, and can get the eggs.

old

run

fox

LESSON XII.

ōld

rŭn

fŏx

ō   ŭ

Can this old fox catch the hen?

The fox can catch the hen, and get the eggs in the nest.

Run, Rab, and catch the fox.

pond

by

feed

Nell

*more words on the next page

ducks

I

them

will

LESSON XIII.

pŏnd   dŭcks   thĕm   fēed

Nĕll

I

bȳ

wĭll

i   ȳ   ck   w

Nell is by the pond.

I see ducks on the pond.

Nell sees the ducks, and will feed them.

She can not get the ducks.

holds to

blind

Mary

hand

kind

LESSON XIV.

hōldṣ   tọ

blīnd   Mā′rў

hǎnd   kīnd

ā   ọ   k   ў

This old man can not see.

He is blind.

Mary holds him by the hand.

She is kind to the old blind man.

LESSON XV.-REVIEW.

I see ducks on the pond; Tom will feed them.

Tom is blind; he holds a box in his hand.

Nell is kind to him.

This old hen has a nest.

Mary will run and get the eggs.

Sue

doll

dress

new

her   let

Sūe   dŏll   drĕss   new   hẽr

lĕt

ẽ

ū

ew

Sue has a doll.

It has a new dress.

She will let Ann hold the doll in her hands, and Ann

will fan it.

Sue is kind to Ann.

there

five

bird

tree

rob   do

thêre

five   bĭrd

trēe   rŏb   do̤

ê   ĩ   v

A bird is in the tree. It has a nest there.

The nest has five eggs in it.

Do not rob the nest.

Will the bird let the cat get her five eggs?

cage

pet

sing

lives

loves   so

LESSON XVIII.

eāġe   ȯ

pĕt

sĭng   ġ

lĭveṣ

sō

lȯveṣ   ng

This is a pet bird.

It lives in a new cage.

It will stand on Sue's hand, and sing.

Sue loves her pet bird.

So do I love it.

are

you

yes

fast

*more words on the next page

too

like

boys

of

play

LESSON XIX.

äre you yĕs fȧst tōo
līke boyṣ ŏf (ŏv) plāy

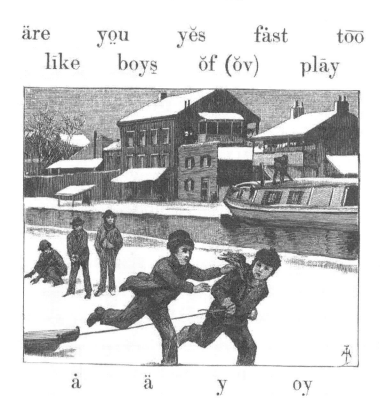

à ä y oy

Do you see the boys at play?

Yes, I see them; there are five of them.

Tom is too fat to run fast.

Nat can catch him.

I like to see boys play.

42

LESSON XX.-REVIEW.

Sue has a doll and a pet bird.

Her doll has a new dress and a cap.

Sue loves Mary, and will let her

hold the doll.

The pet bird lives in a cage. Sue and
Mary will stand by the cage, and the bird
will sing.

There are birds in the tree by the pond.
Can you see them?

Yes; there are five of them in a nest.

Tom will not rob a bird's nest. He is too
kind to do so.

day

what

owl

but

eyes

*more words on the next page

best

well

big

an

night

LESSON XXI.

whạt

owl

ăn

wĕll

ēyeṣ

nīght

dāy

bŭt

bĭḡ

bĕst

ạ   ow   wh

What bird is this? It is an owl.

What big eyes it has!

Yes, but it can not see well by day.

The owl can see best at night.

Nat Pond has a pet owl.

cows

off

our

hot

*more words on the next page

they

come

grass

shade

barn

LESSON XXII.

grāss   theฺy   ċome   ŏff   bärn
shāde   hŏt
ċowṣ   our

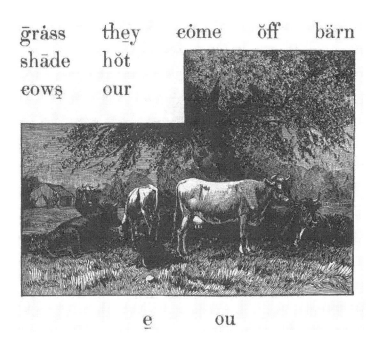

ẹ   ou

The day is hot.

The cows are in the shade of the big tree.

They feed on the new grass.

Our cows do not run off.

At night they come to the barn.

soon

sun

set

neck

*more words on the next page

way

bell

one

their

LESSON XXIII.

soon   sŭn

nĕck   sĕt

way   bĕll   one (wŭn)   thêir

                 o͞o

The sun will soon set.

The cows are on their way to the barn.

One old cow has a bell on her neck.

She sees our dog, but she will not run.

Our dog is kind to the cows.

ship

men

save

rock

*more words on the next page

if
brave
boat
drown

LESSON XXIV.

brāve	ĭf	shĭp	bōat
drown	mĕn	rŏck	sāve

The ship has run on a rock.

Five men are on the ship.

If the boat can not get to them, they will drown.

The boat has brave men in it. They will save the five

men.

LESSON XXV.--REVIEW.

Come, boys, and feed the cows. The sun has set, and they are at the barn.

Sue has a bell on the neck of her pet cat.

One hot day Ann and Nell sat on the grass in the shade of a big tree. They like to rock their dolls, and sing to them.

The brave men in our boat are on their way to the ship. They will save the men in the ship, if they can. They will not let them drown.

What bird has big eyes? The owl. Can an owl see at night? Yes, an owl can see best at night.

fall

ice

cry

did

*more words on the next page

had

with

skates

stone

LESSON XXVI.

fąll	īçe	skātes	erȳ
wĭth	hăd	stōne	dĭd

ą   ç   sk

The boys are on the ice with their skates.

There is a stone on the ice.

One boy did not see it, and has had a fall.

But he is a brave boy, and will not cry.

look

John

all

here

*more words on the next page

mill

have

go

round

wheel

LESSON XXVII.

Look! there are John and Sue by the mill pond.

They like to see the big wheel go round.

They have come to play on the logs and in the boat.

John and Sue will play here all day.

Jane

some

girls

roll

*more words on the next page

or
floor
which
black

LESSON XXVIII.

ôr	Jāne	gĭrlş	flōor
rōll	sȯme	whĭch	blăck

ô

Here are some girls with skates; but they are not on the ice.

Their skates roll on the floor. Which way do you like to skate,--on the ice, or on the floor?

The girl with the new black dress is Jane Bell.

for

hurt

out

how

try

*more words on the next page

cars

be

horse

as

should

LESSON XXIX.

fôr   out   ăṣ   how   trȳ
hôrse   shọuld   hûrt   eärṣ   bē

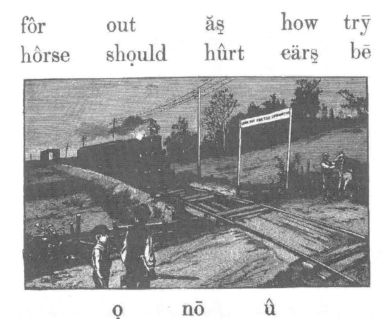

ọ   nō   û

Look out for the cars!

How fast they come!

No horse can go as fast as the cars.

I will not try to catch them, for I should fall and
be hurt.

See the horse look at the cars.

Will he not run?

LESSON XXX.-REVIEW.

There is ice on the pond, and the mill wheel cannot go round.

The boys are all out on the ice with their skates.

I will let you and Tom try to skate; but do not fall, for you will be hurt.

Look! here come the cars.

John and Nat try to skate as fast as the cars go, but they can not. John has had a fall.

The girls are not on the pond; but some of them have skates which roll on the floor.

cut

ax

pile

saw

*more words on the next page

work

Ned

hard

wood

think

LESSON XXXI.

wŏrk   ăx   pīle   Nĕd   thĭnk

wŏŏd   sąw

härd   eŭt

õ   th   ṇ

Ned and John are hard at work. John has a saw,

and Ned has an ax.

They will try to cut all of the wood

which you see in the pile.

Do you think they can do this in one day?

gone

air

hear

two

*more words on the next page

May
cool
noise
walk

LESSON XXXII.

noiṣe âir hēar
ḡŏne Māy wạlk
co͞ol twọ
â oi

Two girls have gone out for a walk.

It is May, and the air is cool. They hear the birds

sing in the trees, and they hear the noise

of the frogs in the pond.

They see men at work and boys at play.

Lesson 33

pull

cart

ride

up

*more words on the next page

hill

goats

Bess

LESSON XXXIII.

pull   cärt   gōats   Bĕss

ŭp   rīde   hĭll

ṳ

Bess has a cart and two goats.

She likes to ride in her cart.

See how the goats pull!

Bess is so big, I think she should walk up the hill.

The goats love Bess, for she feeds them,

and is kind to them.

put

yet

call

ring

*more words on the next page

roof

we

fire

blaze

house

LESSON XXXIV,

blāze   puṭ   yĕt   house

fīre

rōof

eạll

rĭng

wē

z

This house is on fire.

Look! the roof is in a blaze.

Run, boys, and ring the bell. Call some men

to put out the fire.

We may yet save the house, if we work hard.

LESSON XXXV.-REVIEW.

Bess, do you hear a noise?

Yes, Tom; what is it?

It is the mill by our house; logs are cut there.

How do they cut the logs, Tom,-with an ax?

Not with an ax, Bess; it is too hard work; they cut them with a saw.

May we not go and see the mill at work, Tom?

Yes, I think so. The air is cool, and we can walk in the shade. We should go soon, Bess, or the pile of wood will be gone.

Our two goats and the cart are here, Tom; we can ride to the mill. It is not up hill, and the goats can pull us fast.

keep

that

each

rule

*more words on the next page

good

tells

wants

would

Miss

LESSON XXXVI.

Mĭss   wạnts   wọuld   tĕllṣ

rụle

kēep

g̅o̯od

thăt

ēach

ụ

The girls and boys all love Miss May;

she is so kind to them.

Miss May tells them there is a rule that she

wants them to keep. It is, "Do to each one as you

would like each one to do to you."

This is a good rule, and all boys and girls

should keep it.

child when

church

school

books

slates

sehōōl   chĭld

chûrch   whĕn

bŏŏks

slātes

What kind of house is this?

Do you think it is a schoolhouse, or a church?

It looks like a church, but I think it is a schoolhouse.

I see the boys and girls with their books and slates.

When the bell rings, they will go in.

A good child likes to go to school.

88

Henry

kill

know

seen

me

*more words on the next page

oh

eat

quick

first

quail

quāil

sēen

mē

ēat

knōw

quĭck

kĭll

ōh

fĩrst

Hĕn´rў

qu

"John! come here. Be quick, and tell me what kind of bird this is."

"Do you not know, Henry?"

"Oh, no! what is it?"

"It is a quail."

"It is the first quail I have seen. Is it good to eat?"

"Yes; but I should not like to kill it."

sit

near

shut

crib

dear

blue

Kate

baby

name

Kāte   dēar

nāme   blūe

bā′bў   nēar

shŭt   erĭb

sĭt

Is not this a dear baby in the crib?

Her name is Kate, and she has big, blue eyes.

You can not see her eyes, for they are shut.

Kate is a good baby; but she will cry if she is hurt, or if she is not well.

Bess likes to sit near the baby, and to rock her in the crib.

Henry Black and Ned Bell live near our house. They go to school, and I see them go by each day with their books and slates.

Miss May tells the girls and boys that they should be at the schoolhouse when the bell rings. So Henry walks fast, and is first at school. He is a good boy, and wants to keep the rule of the school.

Ned is not a good boy. I do not think he likes to go to school or to church.

I saw him try to kill a quail with a stone. The quail is too quick a bird for that, and Ned did not hurt it; but I know that a good child would not try to kill a bird.

far

were

sea

tall

*more words on the next page

its

light

high

where

LESSON XLI.

lĭght	fär	ĭts	hīgh
whêre	sēa	tạll	wẽre

The tall house which you see on that high rock is a lighthouse. At night its light is seen far out at sea, and the men on ships can tell where to go.

If it were not for this, they would run on the rocks.

How would you like to live in a lighthouse?

took

wolf

us

wrong

*more words on the next page

my

sheep

more

lambs

watch

LESSON XLII.

wrŏng   wǫlf   ŭs   mȳ   tŏŏk

shēep   mōre

wạtch   lămbş

Let us watch the sheep as they feed on the hills.

They like to eat the new grass.

Do you see my two lambs? I had two more; but an old wolf took them one night.

I love my pet lambs. It would be wrong to hurt them.

head

fun

pipe

snow

*more words on the next page

laugh

mouth

made

LESSON XLIII.

läugh   snōw   hĕad   fŭn
mouth   māde   pīpe

gh (as f)

The boys have made a big snow man.

They have put a tall hat on his head,

and an old pipe in his mouth.

Hear them laugh as they play!

It is good fun for the boys.

They would like to have it snow all day

and all night.

buzz

said

mean

once

*more words on the next page

vine

please

bee

could

sweets

LESSON XLIV,

sweets   mean

please   bee

buzz   vine

could

said (sed)

once (wuns)

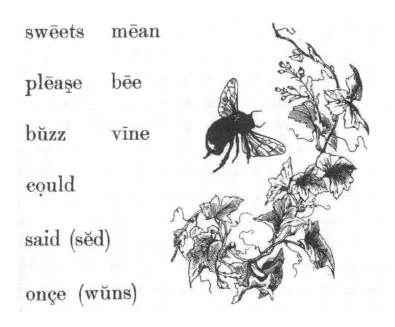

"Buzz! buzz!" a bee said to Mary.

"What do you mean?" said Mary. "Please tell me once more."

"Buzz! buzz! buzz!" but Mary could not tell its wants.

I think it said, "Please let me get some sweets in this vine."

One day Nat and I sat on the high hill by the sea, where the tall lighthouse stands. We could look far out, and could see the ships at sea.

As we sat there, we saw a man near by, with some sheep and lambs. The man had a pipe in his mouth. He sat with us, and let the sheep eat the grass.

What fun it is to see lambs play! It made us laugh to see them.

The man said that once, when the sheep and lambs were out in the snow, an old wolf took one of the lambs, and ran off with it.

I think that men should watch their sheep, so that a wolf cannot catch them.

time

your

done

right

*more words on the next page

while

might

things

halves

LESSON XLVI.

Work while you work,

Play while you play,

One thing each time,

That is the way.

All that you do,

Do with your might,

Things done by halves,

Are not done right.

went

got

fish

safe

*more words on the next page

fell

was

sprang

thank

arms

LESSON XLVII.

wĕnt

fĭsh

fĕll

sāfe

ärmṣ

sprăng   wạṣ   thăṉk   gŏt

One day John went to the pond to fish. His dog, Watch, went with him.

John sat on a log for a time, but did not catch a fish. As he got up to go, he fell off the log.

Watch sprang in to save him. John put his arms round the dog's neck, and was soon safe on the log once more.

"Thank you, my brave old dog," said John to Watch.

then

asks

town

been

*more words on the next page

show

warm

James

drives

James has been to the mill.

The day is warm, and he lets his horse stand

in the shade.

A girl asks him to show her the way to the town. He

tells her the way, and then drives on.

I'll

harm

fur

don't

*more words on the next page

pat

purr

she'll

puss

deeds

I'll   shē'll   dōn't

puss   pûr

păt   fûr

härm   dēeds

I love my dear puss,
Her fur is so warm;
And, if I don't hurt her,
She'll do me no harm.

I'll pat my dear puss,
And then she will purr,
And show me her thanks
For my kind deeds to her.

now

shall

who

queen

*more words on the next page

wreaths

crown

woods

LESSON L.

now   wrēaths   whọ   quēen
woŏds   shăll   crown

It is the first of May. The boys and girls have gone to the woods to have a good time. See them at their play.

The girls have wreaths in their hands. Now they will crown some one Queen of the May. Who shall it be?

It should be the best girl, and that is Kate.

from

God

moon

nut

*more words on the next page

long

ago

small

world

shine

Gŏd   smạll   frŏm

wõrld   mōon

shīne   nŭt

lŏng   a gō′

Do you see that tall tree? Long ago it sprang up from a small nut.

Do you know who made it do so?

It was God, my child. God made the world and all things in it. He made the sun to light the day, and the moon to shine at night.

God shows that he loves us by all that he has done for us. Should we not then love him?

nigh

say

tears

woes

joys

*more words on the next page

smile

griefs

stars

morn

Lord

When the stars, at set of sun,

Watch you from on high;

When the light of morn has come,

Think the Lord is nigh.

All you do, and all you say,

He can see and hear;

When you work and when you play,

Think the Lord is near.

All your joys and griefs he knows,

Sees each smile and tear;

When to him you tell your woes,

Know the Lord will hear.

Continue with one lesson a day. There are no longer sight words to practice. You will read the words at the top of the lesson to your child while pointing them out. Have your child read the words to you. Then let your child read the lesson story to you.

Continue to help your child with a word by using the pictures, beginning sounds and similar words (ie. cat, mat). It's okay to give your child a word or two when he or she is stuck. They are practicing the word when they see it and hear you say it.

MCGUFFEY'S®
First

ECLECTIC READER

Revised Edition

McGuffey Edition and Colophon are Trademarks of

JOHN WILEY & SONS, INC.
NEW YORK · CHICHESTER · WEINHEIM · BRISBANE · SINGAPORE – TORONTO

Review the names and sounds of all the letters.

THE ALPHABET.

A	a	N	n
B	b	O	o
C	c	P	p
D	d	Q	q
E	e	R	r
F	f	S	s
G	g	T	t
H	h	U	u
I	i	V	v
J	j	W	w
K	k	X	x
L	l	Y	y
M	m	Z	z

LESSON I.

dŏḡ   the   răn

ă   ŏ   n   d   ḡ   r   th

dog   the   ran

The dog.

The dog ran.

eăt   măt   ĭ꜀   ŏn

e   t   ĭ   m   ꜀

cat   mat   is   on

The cat.   The mat.

Is the cat on the mat?

The cat is on the mat.

it his pen hand a has man in

The man.   A pen.

The man has a pen.

Is the pen in his hand?

It is in his hand.

hĕn
făt
răt
bŏx

bĭḡ   rŭn   frŏm   eăn

f   b   x   ŭ

big   hen   fat   rat   box   run   from   can

A fat hen.   A big rat.

The fat hen is on the box.

The rat ran from the box.

Can the hen run?

Răb   Ann   hăt   eătch   sēe
ē   ch   s

Rab   Ann   hat   catch   see

See Rab!   See Ann!

See!   Rab has the hat.

Can Ann catch Rab?

136

shē   păt   tōo   now

lĕt   mē

sh   ōo   ow   l

she pat too now let me

Ann can catch Rab.

See! She has the hat.

Now Ann can pat Rab.

Let me pat Rab, too.

will a black hen the nest

w ck

Ned eggs left fed nest
them get will black hen

Ned has fed the hen.

She is a black hen.

She has left the nest.

See the eggs in the nest!

Will the hen let Ned get them?

138

hĕad   hē   Năt

eȯme   wĭth   ănd

ȯ

head   he   Nat   come   with   and

Let me get the black hat.

Now Ned has it on his head,

and he is a big man.

Come, Nat, see the big man with his black hat.

Ned is on the box. He has a pen in his hand. A big rat is in the box. Can the dog catch the rat?

Come with me, Ann, and see the man with a black hat on his head.

The fat hen has left the nest. Run, Nat, and get the eggs.

Nĕll sȯme

păn hĭm

yĕs dọ

yọu hăve

I tọ

ī y v ọ

Nell   some   pan   him   yes

do   you   have   I   to

Do you see Nell?

Yes; she has a pan with some eggs in it.

Let me have the pan and the eggs, will you, Nell?

Has the black hen left the nest?

I will now run to catch Rab. Will you run, too?

O	whĭp	Bĕn
ŭp	stĭll	sĭt
ĭf	stănd	Jĭp

ō　wh　j

O　whip　Ben　up　still　sit　if　stand　Jip

O Ben! let me get in, will you?

Yes, if you will sit still.

Stand still, Jip, and let Ann get in.

Now, Ben, hand me the whip.

Get up, Jip!

1,2.

Kĭt′tў
nīçe
swēet
sĭng
jŭst
hăng
cāġe
thĕn

sŏng   pĕt   pụt   nŏt

k ġ ç ā ў ng ụ

Kitty   nice   sweet   sing   just   hang

cage   then   song   pet   put   not

Kitty has a nice pet. It can sing a sweet song.

She has just fed it.

She will now put it in the cage, and hang the cage up.

Then the cat cannot catch it.

Tŏm tŏp Kĭt′tў′ş

ăt

băck

lŏŏk

gōŏd dŏll thĭnk spŏt

th n̲ ŏŏ

Tom top Kitty's at back

look good doll think spot

Look at Tom and his dog. The dog has a black spot on his back. Do you think he is a good dog?

Tom has a big top, too. It is on the box with Kitty's doll.

sun   we   how   pond   stop   for   go
swim   her   us   hot   duck

The sun is up. The man has fed the black hen

and the fat duck.

Now the duck will swim in the pond. The hen

has run to her nest.

Let us not stop at the pond now, for it is hot.

See how still it is! We will go to see Tom and his top.

LESSON XV.

John   rock   set   jump   fun   must   may

under   skip   bank   but   touch

O John! the sun has just set. It is not hot, now. Let us run and jump. I think it is fun to run, and skip, and jump.

See the duck on the pond! Her nest is up on the bank, under the rock. We must not touch the nest, but we may look at it.

The sun has set, and the pond is still.

John, Ned, Ben, Tom, and Nell stand on the bank, and look at the duck.

The dog with a black spot on his back, is with Tom. See! Tom has his hat in his hand. He has left his big top on the box.

Kitty's doll is on the rock.

Nell has put her pet in the cage. It will sing a sweet song. The duck has her nest under the rock.

It is not hot now. Let us run, and skip, and jump on the bank. Do you not think it is fun?

Kate   old   no   grass   dear   likes   be

drink   milk   cow   out   gives

O Kate! the old cow is in the pond: see her drink! Will she not come out to get some grass?

No, John, she likes to be in the pond. See how still she stands!

The dear old cow gives us sweet milk to drink.

mam mä′   lärġe   ăṣ   pa pä

ärmṣ   rīde   fär   bärn

bōth   Prĭnçe   trŏt   yọur

mamma   large   as   papa   arms   ride

far   barn   both   Prince   trot   your

Papa, will you let me ride with you on Prince?
I will sit still in your arms.

See, mamma! We are both on Prince. How large he is!

Get up, Prince! You are not too fat to trot as far as the barn.

ŏf (ŏv)   thăt   tŏss   fạll

wĕll   Făn′nў   bạll   wạll

wạṣ   pret′tў (prĭt-)   dȯne   whạt

ạ   ạ

of   that   toss   fall   well   Fanny

ball   wall   was   pretty   done   what

O Fanny, what a pretty ball!

Yes; can you catch it, Ann?

Toss it to me, and see. I will not let it fall.

That was well done.
Now, Fanny, toss it to the top of the wall, if you can.

150

hăd   wĕnt   ça̤ll   mīght

flăḡ   nēar   swăm   swĭng

had   went   call   might   flag

near   swam   swing

Did you call us, mamma?

I went with Tom to the pond. I had my doll, and

Tom had his flag.

The fat duck swam to the bank, and

we fed her. Did you think we might fall into the pond?

We did not go too near, did we, Tom?

May we go to the swing, now, mamma?

here   band   hear   horse   play   they

pass   where   front   fine   hope   comes

Here comes the band! Shall we call
mamma and Fanny to see it?

Let us stand still, and hear the men play as they pass.

I hope they will stop here and play for us.

See the large man in front of the band, with his big hat.

What has he in his hand? How fine he looks!

Look, too, at the man on that fine horse.

If the men do not stop, let us go with them and

see where they go.

Bĕss   hăp′pў   māke   cärt

tĕnt   wŏŏds   lĭt′tle   vĕr′ў

bĕd   Rŏb′ert   g̅ŏne   draw

Bess   happy   make   cart   tent   woods

little   very   bed   Robert   gone   draw

Bess and Robert are very happy;

papa and mamma have gone to the woods with them.

Robert has a big tent and a flag,

and Bess has a little bed for her doll.

Jip is with them.

Robert will make him draw Bess and her doll in the cart.

153

Jāmeṣ

mād̄e

mȳ

spōrt

lăp

dŏll'ṣ

said (sĕd)

Mā'rў̆

săng

lāy

spād̄e

dĭḡ

sănd

ȳ

James   Mary   made   sang   my   lay   sport

spade   lap   dig   doll's   sand   said

"Kate, will you play with me?" said James. "We will dig in the sand with this little spade. That will be fine sport."

"Not now James" said Kate; "for I must make my doll's bed. Get Mary to play with you."

James went to get Mary to play with him. Then Kate made the doll's bed.

She sang a song to her doll, and the doll lay very still in her lap.

Did the doll hear Kate sing?

its   shade   brook   picks   all
by   help   stones   glad   soft

Kate has left her doll in its little bed, and has gone to play with Mary and James. They are all in the shade, now, by the brook.

James digs in the soft sand with his spade, and Mary picks up little stones and puts them in her lap.

James and Mary are glad to see Kate. She will help them pick up stones and dig, by the little brook.

"What shall we do?" said Fanny to John. "I do not like to sit still. Shall we hunt for eggs in the barn?"

"No" said John; "I like to play on the grass. Will not papa let us catch Prince, and go to the big woods?"

"We can put the tent in the cart, and go to some nice spot where the grass is soft and sweet."

"That will be fine," said Fanny. "I will get my doll, and give her a ride with us."

"Yes," said John, "and we will get mamma to go, too. She will hang up a swing for us in the shade."

pēep   whīle
tāke   slēep

tŭck   sāfe   ōh   wĕt   fēet
chĭck   càn't   fēelṣ   wĭng

peep while take sleep tuck safe oh
wet feet chick can't feels wing

Peep, peep! Where have you gone, little chick? Are you lost? Can't you get back to the hen?

Oh, here you are! I will take you back. Here, hen, take this little chick under your wing.

Now, chick, tuck your little, wet feet under you, and go to sleep for a while.

Peep, peep! How safe the little chick feels now!

wĭnd   tīme   thêre   fĕnçe

kīte   hīgh   eȳeṣ   brīght

flieṣ   whȳ   dāy   shīneṣ

wind   time   there   fence   kite   high
eyes   bright   flies   why   day   shines

This is a fine day. The sun shines bright. There is a good wind, and my kite flies high. I can just see it.

The sun shines in my eyes; I will stand in the shade of this high fence.

Why, here comes my dog! He was under the cart. Did you see him there?

What a good time we have had! Are you not glad that we did not go to the woods with John?

wĭsh	flōat	tie	knōw
rōpe	bōat	trȳ	shōre
ḡĭve	pōle	dō n't	pụsh
drăḡ	wōn't	ōar	fŭn'nȳ

wish float tie know rope boat try won't oar
shore give pole don't push drag funny

"Kate, I wish we had a boat to put the dolls in. Don't you?"

"I know what we can do. We can get the little tub, and tie a rope to it, and drag it to the pond. This will float with the dolls in it, and we can get a pole to push it from the shore."

"What a funny boat, Kate! A tub for a boat, and a pole for an oar! Won't it upset?"

"We can try it, Nell, and see."

"Well you get the tub, and I will get a pole and a rope. We will put both dolls in the tub, and give them a ride."

bound   Rōṣe   eạlled   g̅ŏt

drown   found   brāve   eāme

Pŏn′tō   jŭmped   mouth

a round′   brôught   wạ′ter

bound   Rose   called   got   drown   found   brave   came
water   Ponto   jumped   mouth   around   brought

"Here, Ponto! Here, Ponto!" Kate called to her dog. "Come, and get the dolls out of the pond."

Rose went under, but she did not drown. Bess was still on the top of the water.

Ponto came with a bound, and jumped into the pond. He swam around, and got Bess in his mouth, and brought her to the shore.

Ponto then found Rose, and brought her out, too.

Kate said, "Good, old Ponto! Brave old dog!"

What do you think of Ponto?

160

June   Lucy   air   kind   trees   singing
blue   when   pure   says   sky   picnic

What a bright June day! The air is pure. The sky is as blue as it can be.

Lucy and her mamma are in the woods. They have found a nice spot, where there is some grass.

They sit in the shade of the trees, and Lucy is singing.

The trees are not large, but they make a good shade.

Lucy's kind mamma says that they will have a picnic when her papa can get a tent.

James and Robert have gone into the shade of a high wall to play ball.

Mary and Lucy have come up from the pond nearby, with brave old Ponto, to see them play.

When they toss the ball up in the air, and try to catch it, Ponto runs to get it in his mouth.

Now the ball is lost. They all look for it under the trees and in the grass; but they cannot see it. Where can it be?

See! Ponto has found it. Here he comes with it. He will lay it at little Lucy's feet, or put it in her hand.

boy our spoil hurrah own coil noise fourth
such join thank about hoist pay July playing

"Papa, may we have the big flag?" said James.

"What can my little boy do with such a big flag?"

"Hoist it on our tent, papa. We are playing Fourth of July."

"Is that what all this noise is about? Why not hoist your own flags?"

"Oh! they are too little."

"You might spoil my flag."

"Then we will all join to pay for it. But we will not spoil it, papa."

"Take it, then, and take the coil of rope with it."

"Oh! thank you. Hurrah for the flag, boys!"

câre	al'wāy₂	līne	Frăṉk
rōw	been (bĭn)	kēeps	hōme

care   always   line   Frank   row   been   keeps   home

Frank has a pretty boat. It is white, with a black line near the water.

He keeps it in the pond, near his home. He always takes good care of it.

Frank has been at work in the garden, and will now row a while.

LESSON XXXVII.

much   one   yet   hungry   seen   grandma   corn   would

"What is that?" said Lucy, as she came out on the steps. "Oh, it is a little boat! What a pretty one it is!"

"I will give it to you when it is finished," said John, kindly. "Would you like to have it?"

"Yes, very much, thank you, John. Has grandma seen it?"

"Not yet; we will take it to her by and by. What have you in your pan, Lucy?"

"Some corn for my hens, John; they must be very hungry."

165

mär′ket   brĕad

bȧs′ket   bôught

mēat

tēa

trȳ′ing

tĕll

whĭch

market   bread   basket   bought

meat   tea   trying   tell   which

James has been to market with his mamma.

She has bought some bread, some meat, and some tea, which are in the basket on her arm.

James is trying to tell his mamma what he has seen in the market.

166

rēads   sō   weârs   plēaṣe

coụld   hâir

fàst   lŏve

ēaṣ'ў   ḡrāy

châir   whọ

ḡlàss'eṣ

reads so wears please could hair fast
love easy gray chair who glasses

See my dear, old grandma in her easy-chair! How gray her hair is! She wears glasses when she reads.

She is always kind, and takes such good care of me that I like to do what she tells me.

When she says, "Robert, will you get me a drink?" I run as fast as I can to get it for her. Then she says, "Thank you, my boy."

Would you not love a dear, good grandma, who is so kind? And would you not do all you could to please her?

does   wonder   mother   other
bee   honey   listen   flower

"Come here, Lucy, and listen! What is in this flower?"

"O mother! it is a bee. I wonder how it came to be shut up in the flower!"

"It went into the flower for some honey, and it may be it went to sleep. Then the flower shut it in."

"The bee likes honey as well as we do, but it does not like to be shut up in the flower."

"Shall we let it out, Lucy?"

"Yes; then it can go to other flowers, and get honey."

bĕst	hĭtched	thêir	shǫuld
ôr	rīd′ing	lĭve	hōldṣ
hāy	drĭv′ing	tīght	ĕar′lў

best hitched their should or riding
live holds hay driving tight early

Here come Frank and James White. Do you know where they live?

Frank is riding a horse, and James is driving one hitched to a cart. They are out very early in the day. How happy they are!

See how well Frank rides, and how tight James holds the lines!

The boys should be kind to their horses. It is not best to whip them. When they have done riding, they will give the horses some hay or corn.

lŏŏk′ing   thôught   pĭck′ing

hẽard

wẽre

sẽarch

yoŭng

lŏved

chĭrp

tōld

dēar′lў

gīrl

bĭrdş

chĭl′dren   be sīdeş′

looking   thought   picking   heard

chirp   were   told   search   dearly

young   girl   loved   birds   children   besides

A little girl went in search of flowers for her mother. It was early in the day, and the grass was wet. Sweet little birds were singing all around her.

And what do you think she found besides flowers? A nest with young birds in it.

While she was looking at them, she heard the mother bird chirp, as if she said, "Do not touch my children, little girl, for I love them dearly."

The little girl now thought how dearly her own mother loved her. So she left the birds. Then picking some flowers, she went home, and told her mother what she had seen and heard.

eight   ask   after   town   past   ah   ticket
right   half   two   train   ding   lightning

"Mamma, will you go to town?"

"What do you ask for a ticket on your train?"

"Oh! we will give you a ticket, mamma."

"About what time will you get back? "

"At half past eight."

"Ah! that is after bedtime. Is this the fast train?"

"Yes, this is the lightning train."

"Oh! that is too fast for me."

"What shall we get for you in town, mamma?"

"A big basket, with two good little children in it."

"All right! Time is up! Ding, ding!"

school   ē′ven (ē′vn)   thrēe

rōom   small

bŏok   tēach′er   nōon

rude   rēad′ing   pōor

school   even   three   room   small   book

teacher   noon   rude   reading   poor

It is noon, and the school is out. Do you see the children at play? Some run and jump, some play ball, and three little girls play school under a tree.

What a big room for such a small school! Mary is the teacher. They all have books in their hands, and Fanny is reading. They are all good girls, and would not be rude even in playing school. Kate and Mary listen to Fanny as she reads from her book.

What do you think she is reading about? I will tell you. It is about a poor little boy who was lost in the woods.

When Fanny has finished, the three girls will go home. In a little while, too, the boys will give up their playing.

apple mew tease cracker down new silly Poll
asleep wants calls knew friends upon flew Polly

Lucy has a new pet. Do you know what kind of bird it is? Lucy calls her Polly.

Polly can say, "Poor Poll! Poor Poll! Polly wants a cracker;" and she can mew like a cat.

But Polly and the cat are not good friends. One day Polly flew down, and lit upon the cat's back when she was asleep.

I think she knew the cat would not like that, and she did it to tease her.

When Lucy pets the cat, Polly flies up into the old apple tree, and will not come when she calls her. Then Lucy says, "What a silly bird!"

"Well, children, did you have a nice time in the woods?"

"Oh yes, mother, such a good time! See what sweet flowers we found, and what soft moss. The best flowers are for grandma. Won't they please her?"

"Yes; and it will please grandma to know that you thought of her."

"Rab was such a good dog, mother."

We left him under the big tree by the brook, to take care of the dolls and the basket.

"When we came back, they were all safe. No one could get them while Rab was there."

We gave him some of the crackers from the basket.

"O mother, how the birds did sing in the woods!"

"Fanny said she would like to be a bird, and have a nest in a tree. But I think she would want to come home to sleep."

"If she were a bird, her nest would be her home. But what would mother do, I wonder, without her little Fanny?"

beach   shells   these   seat   waves   going

ever   sea   watch   evening   lazy   side

These boys and girls live near the sea. They have been to the beach. It is now evening, and they are going home.

John, who sits on the front seat, found some pretty shells. They are in the basket by his side.

Ben White is driving. He holds the lines in one hand, and his whip in the other.

Robert has his hat in his hand, and is looking at the horses. He thinks they are very lazy; they do not trot fast.

The children are not far from home. In a little while the sun will set, and it will be bedtime.

Have you ever been at the seaside? Is it not good sport to watch the big waves, and to play on the wet sand?

log   quiet   proud   pulled   fish   stump   river   father

One evening Frank's father said to him, "Frank, would you like to go with me to catch some fish?"

"Yes; may I go? and with you, father? "

"Yes, Frank, with me."

"Oh, how glad I am!"

Here they are, on the bank of a river. Frank has just pulled a fine fish out of the water. How proud he feels!

See what a nice, quiet spot they have found. Frank has the stump of a big tree for his seat, and his father sits on a log nearby. They like the sport.

sled   throw   winter   hurt   ice   cover   Henry   next
skate   ground   mercy   snow   sister   laughing   pair

I like winter, when snow and ice cover the ground. What fun it is to throw snowballs, and to skate on the ice!

See the boys and girls! How merry they are! Henry has his sled, and draws his little sister. There they go!

I think Henry is kind, for his sister is too small to skate.

Look! Did you see that boy fall down? But I see he is not hurt, for he is laughing.

Some other boys have just come to join in the sport. See them put on their skates.

Henry says, that he hopes his father will get a pair of skates for his sister next winter.

paw   po līte′

mēanṣ   ĭṣ n't

spēak   sĩr

shāke   Fī′dō

trĭcks   tēach

dĭn′ner

El′len

bow′wow

paw   polite   means   isn't   speak   sir   shake

Fido   tricks   teach   dinner   Ellen   bowwow

Ellen, do look at Fido! He sits up in a chair, with my hat on. He looks like a little boy; but it is only Fido.

Now see him shake hands. Give me your paw, Fido. How do you do, sir? Will you take dinner with us. Fido? Speak! Fido says, "Bowwow," which means, "Thank you, I will."

Isn't Fido a good dog, Ellen? He is always so polite.

When school is out, I will try to teach him some other tricks.

puss   shĕd

pāin   wāy

stōle   sạw

hĭd   ēat

Hăt′tie

sŭf′fer

sŏr′rÿ

sȯme′thing   cạught   trīed   Nē′rō

puss shed pain way stole saw hid eat Nero
Hattie suffer sorry something caught tried

"O Hattie! I just saw a large rat in the shed; and old Nero tried to catch it."

"Did he catch it, Frank?"

"No; Nero did not; but the old cat did."

"My cat?"

"No, it was the other one."

"Do tell me how she got it, Frank. Did she run after it?"

"No, that was not the way. Puss was hid on a big box. The rat stole out, and she jumped at it and caught it."

"Poor rat! It must have been very hungry; it came out to get something to eat."

"Why, Hattie, you are not sorry puss got the rat, are you?"

"No, I can not say I am sorry she got it; but I do not like to see even a rat suffer pain."

179

roll   build   grandpa   hard   foam   ships
houses   long   sail   break   wooden   blow

Mary and Lucy have come down to the beach with their grandpa. They live in a town near the sea.

Their grandpa likes to sit on the large rock, and watch the big ships as they sail far away on the blue sea. Sometimes he sits there all day long.

The little girls like to dig in the sand, and pick up pretty shells. They watch the waves as they roll up on the beach, and break into white foam.

They sometimes make little houses of sand, and build walls around them; and they dig wells with their small wooden spades.

They have been picking up shells for their little sister. She is too young to come to the beach.

I think all children like to play by the seaside when the sun is bright, and the wind does not blow too hard.

àsked
fōur
nīght
lăd
çĕnts
fĭf'tў

wạnt'ed
Wĭl'lie'ş
răb'bits
eăr'ried
tĕll'ing
màs'ter

asked   wanted   four   Willie's   night   rabbits
lad   carried   cents   telling   fifty   master

One day, Willie's father saw a boy at the market with four little white rabbits in a basket.

He thought these would be nice pets for Willie; so he asked the lad how much he wanted for his rabbits.

The boy said, "Only fifty cents, sir."

Willie's father bought them, and carried them home.

Here you see the rabbits and their little master. He has a pen for them, and always shuts them in it at night to keep them safe.

He gives them bread and grass to eat. They like grass, and will take it from his hand. He has called in a little friend to see them.

Willie is telling him about their funny ways.

181

bush   eŭn′ning   plāçe   shōw
find   brō′ken   ō′ver   brĭng
a ḡain′ (a ḡĕn′)   făs′ten (făs′n)

bush   cunning   place   show   find

broken   over   bring   again   fasten

"Come here, Rose. Look down into this bush."

"O Willie! a bird's nest! What cunning, little eggs! May we take it, and show it to mother? "

"What would the old bird do, Rose, if she should come back and not find her nest?"

"Oh, we would bring it right back, Willie!"

"Yes; but we could not fasten it in its place again. If the wind should blow it over, the eggs would get broken."

182

strong   round   dry   bill   worked
sends   claws   flit   God   spring

"How does the bird make the nest so strong, Willie?"

"The mother bird has her bill and her claws to work with, but she would not know how to make the nest if God did not teach her. Do you see what it is made of?"

"Yes, Willie, I see some horse-hairs and some dry grass. The old bird must have worked hard to find all the hairs, and make them into such a pretty, round nest."

"Shall we take the nest, Rose?"

"Oh no, Willie! We must not take it; but we will come and look at it again, some time."

fĕath′erṣ   a ḡō′   flȳ   wõrm   crŭmb
fēed′ing   ŭḡ′lȳ   ŏff   fēed   brown
ḡuĕss   thĭngṣ

feathers   ago   fly   worm   crumb   feeding
ugly   off   feed   brown   guess   things

"Willie, when I was feeding the birds just now, a little brown bird flew away with a crumb in its bill."

"Where did it go, Rose?"

"I don't know; away off, somewhere."

"I can guess where, Rose. Don't you know the nest we saw some days ago? What do you think is in it now?"

"O Willie, I know! Some little brown birds. Let us go and see them."

(continued on the next page)

184

"All right; but we must not go too near. There! I just saw the old bird fly out of the bush. Stand here, Rose. Can you see?"

"Why, Willie, what ugly little things! What big mouths they have, and no feathers!"

"Keep still, Rose. Here comes the old bird with a worm in her bill. How hard she must work to feed them all!"

LESSON LIX.

whĭs'tle (whĭs'l)

pŏck'et   wĭl'low

nōte	fĭlled	dĕad	sĭck
walk	ĕv'er ў	blew	lāne
lāme	tāk'ing	eāne	tŏŏk

(The reading is on the next page.)

whistle   pocket   willow   note   filled   dead   sick
walk   every   blew   lane   lame   taking   cane   took

One day, when Mary was taking a walk down the lane, trying to sing her doll to sleep, she met Frank, with his basket and cane.

Frank was a poor, little, lame boy. His father and mother were dead. His dear, old grandma took care of him, and tried to make him happy.

Every day, Mary's mother filled Frank's basket with bread and meat, and a little tea for his grandma.

"How do you do, Frank?" said Mary. "Don't make a noise; my doll is going to sleep. It is just a little sick to-day."

"Well, then, let us whistle it to sleep." And Frank, taking a willow whistle out of his pocket, blew a long note.

"Oh, how sweet!" cried Mary. "Do let me try."

turned   face   cried   low   almost
soon   more   cry   once   because

"Yes, Mary, I will give it to you, because you are so good to my grandma."

"Oh! thank you very much." Mary blew and blew a long time. "I can't make it whistle," said she, almost ready to cry.

"Sometimes they will whistle, and sometimes they won't," said Frank. "Try again, Mary."

She tried once more, and the whistle made a low, sweet sound. "It whistles!" she cried.

In her joy, she had turned the doll's face down, and its eyes shut tight, as if it had gone to sleep.

"There!" cried Frank, "I told you the way to put a doll to sleep, is to whistle to it."

(continued on the next page)

"So it is," said Mary. "Dear, little thing; it must be put in its bed now."

So they went into the house. Frank's basket was soon filled, and he went home happy.

LESSON LXI.

stŏŏd	hĭm sĕlf′	flăp′ping	fĭrst
twĕlve	flăpped	wạlked	flăp
o be̱y′	bĕt′ter	Chĭp′pў	fo͞od
stōne	be fōre′	chĭck′enș	kĕpt

stood himself flapping first twelve flapped
walked flap obey better Chippy food
stone before chickens kept

(continued on the next page)

There was once a big hen that had twelve little chickens. They were very small, and the old hen took good care of them. She found food for them in the daytime, and at night kept them under her wings.

One day, this old hen took her chickens down to a small brook. She thought the air from the water would do them good.

When they got to the brook, they walked on the bank a little while. It was very pretty on the other side of the brook, and the old hen thought she would take her children over there.

There was a large stone in the brook: she thought it would be easy for them to jump to that stone, and from it to the other side.

So she jumped to the stone, and told the children to come after her. For the first time, she found that they would not obey her.

She flapped her wings, and cried, "Come here, all of you! Jump upon this stone, as I did. We can then jump to the other side. Come now!"

"O mother! we can't, we can't, we can't!" said all the little chickens.

"Yes you can, if you try," said the old hen. "Just flap your wings, as I did, and you can jump over."

"I am flapping my wings," said Chippy, who stood by himself; "but I can't jump any better than I could before."

chĭrped nĕv′er in dēed′
slōw′lў rē′al lў
brōōd be ḡăn′
dĭd n't
ūse
dōor
bīte
piēçe

chirped never indeed slowly really brood
began didn't use door bite piece

"I never saw such children," said the old hen. "You don't try at all."

"We can't jump so far, mother. Indeed we can't, we can't!" chirped the little chickens.

"Well," said the old hen, "I must give it up." So she jumped back to the bank, and walked slowly home with her brood.

"I think mother asked too much of us," said one little chicken to the others.

"Well, I tried," said Chippy.

"We didn't," said the others; "it was of no use to try."

When they got home, the old hen began to look about for something to eat. She soon found, near the back door, a piece of bread.

(continued on the next page)

So she called the chickens, and they all ran up to her, each one trying to get a bite at the piece of bread.

"No, no!" said the old hen. "This bread is for Chippy. He is the only one of my children that really tried to jump to the stone."

last   slātes   wrīte   wāste
nēat   tāk′en   elēan   lẽarn
rēad′er   pâr′ents   sĕe′ond

last slates write waste neat taken
clean learn reader parents second

(continued on the next page)

We have come to the last lesson in this book. We have finished the First Reader.

You can now read all the lessons in it, and can write them on your slates.

Have you taken good care of your book? Children should always keep their books neat and clean.

Are you not glad to be ready for a new book?

Your parents are very kind to send you to school. If you are good, and if you try to learn, your teacher will love you, and you will please your parents.

Be kind to all, and do not waste your time in school. When you go home, you may ask your parents to get you a Second Reader.

EP Learn to Read: PART 3

You will complete these lessons one page at a time unless there are directions on the page to continue on to the following page.

The biggest thing to remember is that now you are reading by the sounds of the letters. It will take some getting used to. For instance "me" will not sound like the word which refers to myself. It will sound like "me" in "met."

Your child can be reading for fun outside of these lessons. Early reader books are good choices for building fluency and confidence. Your child might surprise you though and pick up a children's novel and be successful in reading it!

a e i o u

u o i e a

e o a i u

o i e u a

i a u e o

Have your child read the short vowel sounds of the letters, NOT their names. Read "a" as in "hat," "e" as in "bed," "i" as in "hit," "o" as in "hot," "u" as in "sun." This is how you will read these vowels in the coming lessons as well.

Bb

b	a	ba
b	e	be
b	i	bi
b	o	bo
b	u	bu

Have your child say the B sound "buh", then the short vowel sound, then the two together. Don't read "be" as in "bee"; read "be" as in "bed."

Dd

Remember to read the vowels with their short vowel sound. Don't read "do" as in "doo"; read "do" as in "dot"

d	a	da
d	e	de
d	i	di
d	o	do
d	u	du

ba   di   bu   de   bo

Ff

f	a		fa
f	e		fe
f	i		fi
f	o		fo
f	u		fu

ba   fi   di   bu   fe

do   de   bo   fu

da   fo   be

Gg

g	a		ga
g	e		ge
g	i		gi
g	o		go
g	u		gu

gu fu gi bu fe do
ba di fo du

b u bu g bug

Hh

h	a		ha
h	e		he
h	i		hi
h	o		ho
h	u		hu

ga hu fi bu he da bo hi
ba gu fo ha fa gi ho de

h   a   ha   d   had

h   u   hu   g   hug

Jj

j	a		ja
j	e		je
j	i		ji
j	o		jo
j	u		ju

ja	hu	fi	bu	he	da	bo
fu	ga	jo	do	gu	fo	ji

j	o	jo	b	job

j	e	je	t	jet

Kk

k	a		ka
k	e		ke
k	i		ki
k	o		ko
k	u		ku

ka	ju	fi	ku	he	di	ko
gu	da	ke	jo	bu	bo	ki

k	i	ki	d	kid

Ll

l	a	la
l	e	le
l	i	li
l	o	lo
l	u	lu

li	ju	fe	la	ha	di	lu
du	ba	le	jo	ku	go	lo

l	o	lo	g	log
l	e	le	g	leg
l	i	li	p	lip

Mm

m	a		ma
m	e		me
m	i		mi
m	o		mo
m	u		mu

| di | mu | fe | le | ma | bi | la |
| gu | fa | mi | jo | me | bo | mo |

| m | a | ma | d | mad |

| m | o | mo | p | mop |

Nn

n	a		na
n	e		ne
n	i		ni
n	o		no
n	u		nu

ni	hu	de	nu	ma	bi	ha
gu	na	mi	jo	ne	lo	no

n	o	no	d	nod

n	e	ne	t	net

Pp

p	a		pa
p	e		pe
p	i		pi
p	o		po
p	u		pu

na	lu	pe	nu	ba	pi	he
fu	pa	mi	po	du	lo	pu

p	a	pa	n	pan

p	o	po	t	pot

Rr

r	a		ra
r	e		re
r	i		ri
r	o		ro
r	u		ru

da	ru	ge	nu	ra	ji	re
ku	pa	ri	ho	bu	ro	fu

r	a	ra	g	rag

r	i	ri	p	rip

Ss

s	a		sa
s	e		se
s	i		si
s	o		so
s	u		su

sa	ra	se	mu	na	jo	fe
lu	ja	si	hu	su	so	ki

s	a	sa	d	sad

s	i	si	t	sit

Tt

t	a		ta
t	e		te
t	i		ti
t	o		to
t	u		tu

ha	ta	le	tu	ma	bo	je
su	na	ti	hu	gu	to	ki

t	i	ti	p	tip
t	a	ta	g	tag

Vv

v	a		va
v	e		ve
v	i		vi
v	o		vo
v	u		vu

va	sa	ve	tu	da	vo	gi
tu	fa	vi	du	vu	ro	li

v   a   va   n   van

Ww

w	a		wa
w	e		we
w	i		wi
w	o		wo
w	u		wu

vi	wa	be	si	fa	do	wi
wu	ga	hi	we	vu	wo	lo

w	i	wi	n	win

w	e	we	t	wet

Yy

y	a		ya
y	e		ye
y	i		yi
y	o		yo
y	u		yu

yi	ga	de	ni	ra	yu	ti
mu	ya	li	ye	vu	yo	ki

y   a   ya   p   yap

Zz

z	a	za
z	e	ze
z	i	zi
z	o	zo
z	u	zu

pi	za	me	zi	zo	du	ti
ru	sa	fi	ze	vu	yo	zu

z	i	zi	p	zip

Bb

bad   bag   bam   bat

bed   beg   Ben   bell   bet

bid   big   bin   bit   biz

bob   bog   bop

bud   bug   bun   bum   bus   but

buzz

Dd

dab   dad   dam

den

did   dig   dim   dip

dog   dop   dot

dub   dud   dug

Ff

fab fad fan fat

fed fell

fib fig fill fin fit fizz

fog

fun fuzz

Gg

gab gag gal gap

get

gill

gob God got

gun gut

Hh

had   ham   hat
hen   hell
hid   hill   him   hip   hit
hog   hop   hot
hug   hut

Ll

lab   lad   lag   lap
led   leg   let   less
lid   lip   lit
log   lop   lot
lug

Mm

mad   man   map   mat

men   met

mid   mill   miss

mob   mom   mop

mud   mug   mutt

Nn

nab   nag   nap

Ned   net

nip

nod   not

nut

Pp

pad　pan　pal　pat
peg　pen　pep　pet
pig　pill　pin　pit
pod　pop　pot
pub　pun　pup

Rr

rad　rag　ran　rap　rat
red
rib　rid　rig　rim　rip
rob　rod　rot
rub　rug　run　rut

Ss

sad sag sap sat

sell set

sin sip sit

sob sop

sub sun sum sup

Tt

tab tad tag tan tap

Ted tell ten

tin tip

tot

tub tug

Vv

van   vet

Ww

wag   wet   win

Yy

yap   yet

Zz

zig   zag   zap

bad had lad mad pad sad tad

ban can Dan fan pan ran tan

bat cat fat hat mat pat rat sat vat

Ben den hen men pen ten

bet get met net pet set

bid did hid lid kid rid

bin fin pin sin tin

bit fit hit mitt pit sit wit

bop cop hop lop mop sop top

dot got hot lot pot rot tot

bun fun gun pun run sun

but cut gut hut nut mutt rut

bad lid	had hen	mad Dan	sad Ben
ban sin	can hop	fan men	cop ran
bat top	cat hid	fat pet	wet hat
hit mat	pat kid	mutt sat	got rat
hot pen	ten men	rat bit	hid rot
get pot	met tot	men hop	pet rat
hid top	did hop	cut lid	hot sun
hid nut	hot lid	hit gut	fun hut
hot bun	got mop	men run	fit man

After this point the font will change to make sure the capital letter "I" is distinguished from the lowercase letter "l."

I met a dog.
I met a fun dog.
I met a fun, fat dog.
I met a fun, fat, wet dog.
I met Sam, a fun, fat, wet dog.

I fed a cat.
I fed a hot cat.
I fed a hot, mad cat.
I fed a hot, mad cat a bit.

I can sit.
I can sit and hop.
I can sit, hop and run.
I can sit, hop, run and jog.

C, K

c a ca cap cat can
k e ke Ken keg
k i ki kid kit kiss
c o co cod cop cot
c u cu cup cut

cut cap   can cut   kiss Ken
cop cup   cat cot   cod kit

CK

pack deck sick sock buck
rack peck tick rock duck
sack neck pick tock muck
back deck lick lock luck

kiss cat
pick lock
cup sack
cut sock
rock kit
neck cut

back pack hot deck fed duck
tick tock pack hat hot rock

ND

and	sand
band	hand
land	sand and land

end	bend
fend	mend
tend	tend and mend

pond	pond end
fun fund	fund and fend

I am at a big pond.

ST

fast

last

mast

past

best

nest

pest

rest

fist

list

just

must

FT

raft   left   soft
gift   lift   loft
sift   tuft

MP

camp   damp
lamp   ramp
limp   romp
bump   jump
pump   rump

gift lamp   lift ramp   left camp

bump tuft   jump fast   best raft

Jump in the pond.

NT

pant	lint	tent
bent	mint	hunt
rent	punt	tint
sent	runt	went

LT

belt	felt	melt	tilt
hilt	kilt	pelt	wilt

sent felt   melt mint   pant belt

hunt pelt   tilt tent   last sand

The duck is a runt.

I went and felt the sand.

LK

milk   silk   bulk
hulk   sulk

LD

held   meld   weld

held milk   weld bulk   meld silk

silk pant   held gift   list milk

I just held the soft silk.

The list had milk.

LF

elf   self
golf   gulf

LP

help   kelp
gulp   pulp

PT

kept   wept   rapt

kept golf   kelp gulf
self help   pump pulp

The elf wept in the tent.

SK

bask   mask   tisk   musk
task   desk   bask
risk   tusk   disk

SP

gasp   lisp
wisp   rasp

gasp risk   bent desk   milk task
belt held   felt mist   jump raft
bend gift   best melt   lift hand

I ran fast to hand the disk to the man.

If you read these words easily across each row, then read them down each column.

bent	tent	sent	dent	rent
fast	past	last	mast	vast
rest	pest	test	nest	best
bust	dust	rust	must	just
gift	lift	rift	sift	
damp	lamp	camp	ramp	

Y

These words add -y without changing.

sand	sandy
milk	milky
pest	pesty
jump	jumpy

These words change their spelling. How?

fun	funny
sun	sunny
run	runny
mud	muddy
pup	puppy
dad	daddy

Y

silly Bobby
funny Penny
sandy Sammy
fuzzy Andy
muddy buddy
rusty daddy
milky nanny
lumpy kitty
dusty mommy
windy doggy
sunny puppy

The silly puppy can jump and run.

Doubles

Did you notice that we double the end letter to add a –y to the words with only three letters? Here are some other words with double letters.

bell   fell   hell   sell   tell

bill   dill   gill   hill   pill   will

dull   hull   mull

buzz   fuzz   fizz   jazz

buff   cuff   huff   muff   puff

bass   mass   pass   mess   miss   kiss

messy mess   fuzzy fuzz   fizzy fizz

The one below is a little different. The "a" has a different sound. Do you remember how to read the first word, *all*?

all   ball   call   fall   hall   tall

SH

Here are two letters you see together a lot. Do you know what sound they make together? Put your finger to your mouth and let someone know they should be quiet. Sh!

bash	cash
dash	gash
hash	lash
mash	rash
sash	dish
fish	wish
hush	lush
mush	rush

fishy dish	fast cash	funny wish
rush golf	mad dash	Sh! Hush!

The messy fish is wet.

TH

Here are another two letters you see together a lot. To make this sound you have to stick out your tongue!

bath
math
path
Beth
with
Seth

kitty bath   funny math   with cash

Math is fun with EP!

Dash fast on the muddy, buggy path!

CH, TCH

These two letter combos above make the same sound.

bun   bunch
pun   punch
ben   bench
pin   pinch

lunch   such   rich   much

ba   batch   pi   pitch
      match   catch
      patch   fetch
      botch   notch

Fetch his lunch.

Pitch the ball or sit on the bench.

Catch them in the ditch.

bunch	bust	buck	buff	
batch	bash	back	bill	bath
munch	wish	wick	will	with

ditch	dash	dock	dull	duck
lunch	lash	lock	lull	lick
pinch	posh	pack	pill	path
hunch	hash	hack	hill	hunt
ranch	rash	rack	rust	risk
match	mash	muck	math	must

candy is yummy   happy math

windy path   sandy ditch

Watch the sun set in the west.

This dish is rich.

Milk with lunch is best.

ING

d ing   ding
k ing   king
r ing   ring
s ing   sing
th ing   thing

The king can sing.

ANG

b ang   bang
g ang   gang
h ang   hang
r ang   rang
s ang   sang

The gang sang.

UNG

h   ung   hung
r   ung   rung
s   ung   sung

ONG

b   ong   bong
d   ong   dong
l   ong   long
s   ong   song

Sing a long song. I sang a long song.

Hang on a rung. I hung on a rung.

ding dong   ping pong   King Kong

ING

bang	ing	banging
jump	ing	jumping
sing	ing	singing
mash	ing	mashing

ringing	catching
risking	pitching
helping	sending
fishing	packing
itching	hanging

I am jumping and singing.

Ben is pitching. Jen is catching.

Penny is helping and packing.

Fishing in the pond is fun.

INK

l	ink	link
m	ink	mink
p	ink	pink
r	ink	rink
s	ink	sink
w	ink	wink

w ink   wink   ing winking

ANK

b	ank	bank	r	ank	rank
s	ank	sank	t	ank	tank
y	ank	yank	th	ank	thank

I am thinking.
I am thanking Jen.
The bank is pink. The rink is red.

UNK

b	unk	bunk		d	unk	dunk
f	unk	funk		g	unk	gunk
h	unk	hunk		p	unk	punk
s	unk	sunk				

ing	sing	singing
ink	sink	sinking
ank	bank	banking
unk	dunk	dunking
ink	wink	winking
ank	thank	thanking
unk	junk	junking

I am jumping on the bunk bed.

When A Says Its Name

can	cane		hat	hate
tap	tape		Jan	Jane
pan	pane		mad	made

sale   wave   bare   pave   rate

game   gate   name   safe   dare

Notice the spelling on these next ones:

back	bake		lack	lake
sack	sake		rack	rake

made a date   bake a cake

fake name   safe at lake

bake sale   rate the game

thanking Jane   helping rake

red cape   wave hand

When I Says Its Name

bit	bite		dim	dime
fin	fine		hid	hide
kit	kite		rid	ride
win	wine		rip	ripe

Notice the spelling on these:

fill	file		pill	pile
mill	mile		lick	like

life in a mine   ride a kite

Hide nine dimes in a pile.
I like ripe limes.
I like the fine kite I made.
Ride a mile on the lake.

When O Says Its Name

hop   hope   rob   robe
rod   rode   not   note

home   code   poke   nope   woke
hope   lone   cone   rope   pole

Notice the spelling change on these:

doll   dole   jock joke

mole home   hole in robe
vote Dole   note in code

I hope it is a joke.

The mole made a home in the hole.

I woke and rode home.

The pole is in the hole at Mile Lake.

The yummy cone fell at lunch.

When U Says Its Name

cub   cube   cut   cute
us use

See if you can hear the difference between the words above and these words:

tub   tube   duck duke

The second group of words say "oo."
The first group of words say, "yoo."

Say them again and pay attention to the difference. Can you hear it?

rude joke   use tube   cute duke

The duke will rule.
Luke is rude.
Use the tube to cure it.
He fumes if he is mad.
The cute puppy is licking the bone.

When E Says Its Name

We've been adding an "e" to the end of words to make a vowel say its name.

Here are some for E: *here* and *Eve*.

If you have played on Starfall.com, then maybe you know the song, "When two vowels go a walking, the first one does the talking." In other words, when two vowels are together, the first vowel says its name. Here are some examples with E.

bee   beef   beep   beet

Dee   deep   deer

fee   feed   feel   feet

pee   peep   peer

see   seed   seen

wee   weed   week   weep

Please continue with this lesson on the next page.

Those words all had two Es, so it's easy to tell that they say E. Here are words that are spelled, EA. They are two vowels together, so the first one is going to say its name. E comes first so when you see EA, you read the E sound.

bead	beam	beat	
deal	dear		
heal	heap	heat	
lead	leap	lean	
meal	mean	meat	
team	tear	weak	wean

I like eating meat.
The red team is in the lead.

The sentences below use different words that sound the same. Which two words sound the same? Which word is which?

In the heat I feel weak each week.
Dear mom, I see a deer.
I eat a beet. I hear a beat.

When E Says Its Name

Here's another time E says its name, when it's all by itself at the end of a two-letter word. Read these examples:

be   he   me   we   she

The last one is different! It has three letters, but the *s* and *h* only make one sound, right?

I am eating a red beet.

I can hear mine beating.

He will reach home so fast.

He is teaching pitching.

We ride miles on neat bikes.

No, bake a cube cake and feed me it.

Go dig a hole and fill it back in with mud.

(O can do this as well—no, go, so, but not to or do!)

Do not be here late!

When O Says Its Name

Here's a time when O says its name when it is written all by itself. Read these examples:

old	bold	fold	gold
hold	mold	sold	told
bolt	colt	host	most

The lime is old and moldy.

Take hold of his hand.

The most fun is running and jumping.

Fold it and put it here.

It is windy and cold inside!

Hosting him, I am told, is bold.

He mines for gold here.

The colt has fun running fast.

When I Says Its Name

Read these examples where I says its name:

find   hind   kind
mind   mild   wild

Here are two similar examples with I and O:

tiny   pony

The kind, old man is Dan.

The wild, tiny boy is Dave.

His pony is mild and his fish is sick.

His mind is quick and his feet, fast.

Can he find me here in this shop?

Be kind to him.

The moldy roll will make me sick.

I told him kindly to be here at sun up.

Long and Short

Read these examples with words with both the long and short vowel sounds. When the vowel says its name, we call that the long vowel sound.

Will he tell a tall tale?

Hug a cute puppy and kick a tire.

Pop in at home and eat lunch.

His dad has a job at home.

His big kite will win the game.

Sad Sam ate an old, bad date cake.

Sit with me here and sip hot tea.

His cat will gulp a bug in the sun.

It is time, so go and ride home.

The lone kid sits and sits.

At the game, catch the ball in the mitt.

ING

When we added E onto the end of short words like *bit*, making it *bite*, the E made the I say its name.

To make the word bite – ing, we write *biting*. The second vowel makes the first say its name.

But sometimes we don't want the vowel to say its name! To write hug – ing, we write *hugging*. We put in a double letter to keep the vowels apart so the second vowel doesn't make the first vowel says its name.

Read these examples of double letter words:

bed   bedding
bet   betting
fan   fanning
fit   fitting
get   getting
hop   hopping
hum   humming

Please continue with this lesson on the next page.

jig   jigging
let   letting
map   mapping
mop   mopping
pop   popping

The words below don't need an extra letter. Why?

limp   limping
jump   jumping
bump   bumping
help   helping
tell   telling

I like telling time.
I like helping with mopping.

The hopping and jumping game is fun.
I must get the puppy bedding.

ED

Now we are going to take some of these same words and add an ED to the end of them.

These words you say with a "D" sound on the end.

fan	fanning	fanned
hum	humming	hummed
jig	jigging	jigged
bag	bagging	bagged
ban	banning	banned
tan	tanning	tanned

These words you say with a "T" sound on the end.

mop	mopping	mopped
pop	popping	popped
limp	limping	limped
jump	jumping	jumped
bump	bumping	bumped
help	helping	helped
hop	hopping	hopped
map	mapping	mapped

continued...

These words you say with an "ED" sound at the end.

fit	fitting	fitted
melt	melting	melted
bend	bending	bended

He helped with fitting the hat.

I hummed and jigged and then I limped.

He fanned me to make me cold.

I bumped the desk and the milk fell.

ER

Now we are going to take some of these same words and add an ER to the end of them.

fan	fanning	fanned	fanner
hum	humming	hummed	hummer
jig	jigging	jigged	jigger
bag	bagging	bagged	bagger
tan	tanning	tanned	tanner
limp	limping	limped	limper
jump	jumping	jumped	jumper
help	helping	helped	helper
hop	hopping	hopped	hopper
kick	kicking	kicked	kicker

Did you notice all the double letters? They don't all have double letters, which ones do? They *do* all have two letters between the first and second vowel.

Please continue this lesson on the next page.

The bagger bagged the meat and milk.

The tanner tanned the hide of a deer.

I am a helper at home with mom and dad.

The kicker is kicking the ball.

He hummed and ate all the cake.

The fast hopper is the winner.

Lending a hand helps a lot.

Winter is wetter than summer.

ING and ER and ED

Sometimes we want the first vowel to say its name, like with *biting*. We want the I to say its name. If we added a double T, what would it say?

bit-ting – That's not a word!

Read these examples with NO double letters, so all of the first vowels say their name.

bite ing	biting	biter
ride ing	riding	rider
mine ing	mining	miner

mope	moping	moper	moped
vote	voting	voter	voted
rope	roping	roper	roped
hate	hating	hater	hated
rate	rating	rater	rated
rake	raking	raker	raked

Please continue with this lesson on the next page.

read	reading	reader	
lead	leading	leader	
bead	beading	beader	beaded
leap	leaping	leaper	leaped

Reading is fun.

I voted. I like the leader.

Riding fast, we feel the wind go past.

The miner is at his home near the mine.

Long and Short

hop	hopping	hopped
hope	hoping	hoped
mop	mopping	mopped
mope	moping	moped
tap	tapping	tapped
tape	taping	taped
back	backing	backed
bake	baking	baked
fill	filling	filled
file	filing	filed

I am a renter and I rented a home here.

I taped the sheet up to make a tent.

The cake filling is yummy.

I am hoping I am hopping the fastest.

He backed up and fell in the ditch!

He moped all the time.

The rider must help us.

He is lending me a hand by helping to mop.

Summer is sunny and winter is chilly.

Chunk that Word!

You can break up big words and read their parts.

it-self	itself
can-not	cannot
bed-time	bedtime
sun-set	sunset
for-get	forget

sal-a-man-der	salamander

Try these:

cupcake	cup-cake
baseball	base-ball
rabbit	rab-bit
bobbin	bob-bin
talented	tal-en-ted

More than One

ball	balls	wall	walls
bike	bikes	rake	rakes
cat	cats	hat	hats
dog	dogs	mug	mugs
hit	hits	pit	pits
kid	kids	bid	bids
lock	locks	rock	rocks
patch	patches	pitch	pitches
wish	wishes	rash	rashes
buzz	buzzes	fizz	fizzes
lunch	lunches	bunch	bunches

X

box (rhymes with socks)
fox
fix
fax
tax (sounds like tacks)
tux

exit   ex-it
expect   ex-pect

exterminate ex-ter-min-ate

I expect him to fix his box.

I came in the exit!

SH

shut	ship	shape	shop
share	shot	shin	sheep
shell	shack	shade	shake
shall	shame	shave	she
shear	shed	sheet	shelf
Sherry	shift	shine	shellfish

| shock | shocker | shocked | shocking |

| shone | shifted | shifting | shearer |
| shared | shined | shaved | shudder |

The shearer, she shaved the sheep.

The sun is shining, so I am sitting in the shade.

I expect the ship shop to be open.

SH

wash ship   wish shape   dish shop

push shot   sheep sleep   shake fish

sell shell   she gushed   rush shot

Sherry shined   shudder shock

yummy dish   sunny shape

I rushed to the shop; I needed dishes.

The sun shone on the sand and shells.

I am washing my ship.

She's shaping up.

She pushes and pulls and tugs.

I am eating a yummy dish at the Fish Shack.

CH

chips   chop   chapped

chopper   cheep   cheap

cheat   cheer   chat

chatter   chattering   chipping

chipper   chug   chugging

chase   check   checkers

I chased the chopper until I had chapped lips.

Does she cheat at checkers?

I got chips cheap and cheered.

Chopping cheese is his job.

She is chattering to me.

CH

pitch chips
ditch checked

batch chopped
rich and cheap

chase the catcher
much chattering

Chase and catch her.

The teacher checked the tests.

She chops trees for her job.

Run and fetch a bag of chips.

The dish is rich and yummy.

Get shade in the ditch.

Bake a batch of muffins.

Rent a cheap tent to pitch near the lake.

WH

when   wheat   white   whiz

whip   whim   which   whopper

There are some wh words that don't follow the rules we've learned. You should just know them:

why   who   whose   what

where   weather

When did he leave his job?

Which game did she like best?

Whose bike is at home?

What team has a white logo?

Where is the whiz kid who likes math?

Who told that whopper of a tale?

Why is the weather so cold?

TH

then	this	that	those
these	thin	thick	thud
them	there (rhymes with where)		

this, that and the other

These bells sing songs.

This bathtub is deep.

The weather is thick with fog.

Then hand this to them.

Those fans cheer each goal.

There is the thin path that leads home.

The thick mud gets under Beth's feet.

There is an S on the end of Beth's name. There is not more than one Beth. That mark is called an apostrophe. The apostrophe S tells us that the feet belong to Beth. They are Beth's feet.

QU

quick   quit   queen   quite

quilt   quack   quiet (qu – I – et)

I think I hear a duck quacking.

It is quite quiet here.

Quick, let's bake a cake.

I like soft quilts.

I quit thinking bad things.

She is quite wonderful.

Thank Sally for the queen sized quilt.

Review

When is he going to see the queen?

When is the best time to quit?

What is he thinking?

Where is she chasing him so quickly?

The cabin is quiet to rest in.

Rabbits do not quack.

Sherry is chomping on her lunch.

I like this cheese so much!

Let's sit in the shade; the weather is sunny.

Which lake is the best?

L Blends

a	la	bla	blab	blabber
a	la	fla	flap	flapping
a	la	pla	plan	planned
a	la	cla	clap	clapping
a	la	gla	glad	gladden
a	la	sla	slap	slapped

bleed	bleep	blooper	blame
blip	fleet	flame	flip
flop	flute	flume	plod
plume	pluck	plate	plane
clan	clear	plug	plugging

He claps his hands if he is happy.

The duck is flapping its wings.

L Blends

clean	cleaner	cleaned	cleaning
clog	clogger	clogged	clogging
clutch	clear	cleared	clearing
gleam	glum	glob	globbed
slip	slipper	sleep	sleeping
sleet	slug	sled	sledding

slum	slit	slab	slush

I slid in the slush after sledding.

I cleaned it and cleared the glob from the clog.

I plan on making plucked chicken for lunch.

The slug gleamed in the sunny clearing.

L Blends

clean slide	flip flag	glad plan
plug clog	slip slide	glum glad
blame plane	sleep fleet	clip clop
pluck blob	blip bleep	slip shod

| gleaming shine | pleading slob |
| cleaner flame | bleeding Glen |

I am sleepy. Please be quiet so I can go to sleep.

I like flip flops on the sandy beach.

I pluck the weeds near the plants.

I am glad when the sun is shining.

I cleaned there and I need to clean here.

SM, SN

a	ma	sma	smash
e	me	sme	smell

smile   smock   smear   smitten

a	na	sna	snap
o	no	sno	snob

snipe   sneer   snip   snub

I am smitten with the smell of lunch.

The snob sneered at me.

It's a snap to smash a glass.

I smile when I think of him.

She got a smear on her smock.

ST, SP

e	te	ste	step
i	ti	sti	still
o	to	sto	stop
u	tu	stu	stuck
a	pa	spa	spat
e	pe	spe	sped

stick	stale	speed	steed
spine	steer	spade	stiff

I stepped in mud and got stuck.

I steered the clean, speedy rocket.

He smiled and stopped near the spitting llama. (I put in a funny word. Can you guess what it is?)

SC, SK

a can scan
i kit skit

Kate   skate   kill   skill
cat   scat   etch   sketch
kin   skin   cab   scab
scale   skip   scare

He can skip and sketch with skill.

He skated and fell and cut his skin. Then he got a scab.

Kate scared the cat and it scaled the wall.

S

scan	scab	scat
scale	scare	
skit	skin	skip
skill	skate	skill-fully
smile	smell	smash
smock	smear	
snip	snot	snap
snob	snub	
spare	spit	spot
sputter	spud	
stop	stun	stab
steep	still	

I can skillfully sketch in steep spots.

I still skip the scary parts.

R Blends

ra	bra	brass	Brad	bran
ra	cra	crab	cram	crack
ra	dra	drag	drat	drab
re	fre	Fred	fret	fresh
ri	gri	grip	grill	grit
ro	pro	prop	prom	prod

ru	tru	truck	trum-pet-ing

I hear the animals trumpeting.

There is a fox trapped inside the grill.

This truck delivers bricks. (de-liv-ers)

Cracked, fresh crab is yummy.

Drag the brass bed up here.

fan-tas-tic   won-der-ful

R Blends

Clear a spot for me at the trading post.

Be cheerful, not grumpy.

Bring lots of creamy treats, please.

He has a trick up his sleeve.

I like this evening's program.

Grab a blade of green grass.

I am in the bathtub dripping wet.

Black is not the same as white.

We planned a free trip for Fred.

Too much pride is a bad thing.

Grandma told me that creaking bones mean bad weather.

I had a dream that I was a crab.

(The word "was" doesn't follow our rules.)

Review

Glitter is fun to put on crafts.

Slithering snakes like cramped muddy spots. (Sli-ther-ing)

I like to eat snacks between meals.

Bring trunks to pack for the trip to the tropics. (trop-ics)

Greedy kids do not get treats.

Sniff and smell this rose.

Grab a clock and time me!

She pricked her finger and it bled.

Clean the clearing for a picnic.

AR

are   bar   car   far   par   tar
art   bark   card   farm   park   tarp
arm   cart   part   tart
dark   hark   lark   mark   stark   spark
dart   mart   start   smart
darn   yarn   barn   harm

That was sharp! Be careful.

The bug darted here and there.

Tree bark can be made into paper.

He can hear barking on a farm.

Are we going to the park?

Pull the cart along with us.

OR

or   for   ford fork fort form
cord cork pork sort born corn
horn morn torn bore

These sound the same but are AR words:
war wart warm warn
warp ward

Is it going to storm?

He was born in September. (Sep-tem-ber)

The corn is ripe to be picked.

She eats pork with a fork.

A horn is a brass instrument.(in-stru-ment)

I warned her that it was boring.

Sort these socks for me, please.

OR

These sound like OR but are spelled differently:

door   floor   more   score
four   your   roar   soar

This sentence has all six different spellings for OR. Can you find them all?

Four stores get awards for selling boards indoors.

After the storm it will be warmer.

The boring actor wins an award.

Wipe your feet before you step on the floor.

It poured in the morning and I was dripping wet.

We walked north.

ER   IR   UR

These sound the same but are spelled differently:

her	herd	perm	perch
bird	dirt	first	thirst
burn	hurt	purr	turn

The girl got hurt falling in the dirt.

The cat purred when she was thirsty.

A bird sat singing from its perch.

Her farm has a herd of pigs.

Be careful not to get burned.

I got a perm, so my hair is curly.

I finished my chores first.

(We haven't learned the word my yet. Did you figure out that the Y says I?)

More UR Sounds

These words have the same sound in them but are spelled in two different ways.

work   word   worm   world
earth   heard   learn   earn

I think that was the worst I heard!

The early bird gets the worm.

The whole world shares the earth.

I finished my chores first.

The girl learned her words this week.

I heard your song being sung at church.

The card got torn at the park.

See you later alligator.

I earn money being a hard worker.

AI

You learned that ee and ea both say E. Well, the rule that "when two vowels go awalking the first one does the talking" is true for other sounds too. We are first going to look at different ways to make the A sound, to make A say its name. One way is with the letters ai together.

sail	tail	rail	wail
pail	mail	nail	jail
fail	trail	train	rain
pain	gain	main	fair
pair	hair	lair	maid
paid	raid	laid	wait
paint	plain	dainty	faint

Use the pail and paint the plain train rail red.

Deliver the mail quickly to the jail in the rain.

AY

Here's another combination that makes A say its name.

say	ray	may	pay
lay	day	hay	way
away	tray	clay	play
pray	today	holiday	gray

Today is a gray day, but I want to play.

Bring clay on a tray and we'll play.

("We'll" means we will. The apostrophe separates the WE from the Ls. You don't read the word as "well." You read WE and then add the L sound.)

I will pay the way for us on the train.

Let's go away for the holiday.

Pray for a better way.

Saying "please" is polite manners.

She is learning to lay the hay for the animals.

A word to learn with the A sound is th<u>ey</u>.

Long O Sound

Here are some ways that you can write the long O sound, how you can make O say its name.

oat   boat   coat   float   goat
doe   foe   hoe   goes   toe
tow   bow   mow   row   low

I like yellow roses and he likes bows and arrows.

His pillow has boats on it.

The goat eats the grass to mow it!

This floats so slow.

He goes to play with no coat.

Your toes are in a row.

The doe bends low to eat the oats.

The sun's rays light the rainbow.

Long O and A Sounds

Row, row, row your boat, gently up the stream. Merrily, merrily, merrily, merrily, life is but a dream.

Little Bo Peep has lost her sheep!

The wind blows softly and the stream flows slowly.

Wait and stay today to play and paint.

Rain, rain go away.

The boat sails swiftly in the sea.

The jam on his toast stained his shirt.

The soap boat floats in the bath.

Mowing the grass is my chore.

Tomorrow we'll go below deck.

(to – mor –row)

Train tracks   chain cracks   stained stacks

Long U Sound

Two vowels make the first say its name:

true   glue   blue
fruit   juice   suit

Here's a word that does not follow the rule! SHOE

Here are other ways to make the long U sound.

too   soon   spoon   moon
food   tooth   cartoon

Ew!   new   pew   blew
flew   stew   chew   mew

you   soup   group

Eat your fruit stew with a spoon.

Do you think it is true that the suit is blue?

IE

Here is a weird one. Sometimes IE sounds like the letter name E:

field   shield   thief   belief
believe   relieve   Debbie   Katie

You can also see it in some plural words. When a y comes after a vowel we just add an s, like in *day* we write *days* and for *key* we write *keys*. But if the y doesn't come after a vowel, if it comes after a consonant, we write it like this:

party   parties   daisy   daisies
baby   babies   puppy   puppies

The thief stole the daisies for the parties.

The puppies are playing in the field.

I believe a nap will relieve the babies.

He hung the shield up in the lobby for the tourists to see.

IE

Now ie is going to sound the way it should. It is going to make I say its name:

pie   lie   tie

We know y can sound like E, but it can sound like I too.

try   tries   fly   flies
fry   fries   pry   pries
spy   spies

He tries so hard to fly.

Try and pry this pie from the pan.

Never lie.

Eat these yummy cheesy fries.

There is a fly on my tie.

He trapped the thief by spying on him.

I sounds

Here are some more words with the I sound.

my	by	type	style
guy	buy		
rye	bye		
guide			
high	light	night	bright

My guide has weird style.

I like rye and wheat but not oat.

Go spy on that guy.

Why are you so shy?

I believe Debbie tries to type super fast.

Hang the light high so that it will be bright tonight.

My kids are playing hide and seek.

Long Vowel Sounds

The tiny bird tries to fly free in the air. I see its first flight.

Coal is burned in the stove for heat.

This new book has interesting stories.

I believe his daisy field is for sale.

People think that trees grow slowly.

May we please use the guidebook?

The boat will be waiting in the harbor tonight.

Type this word as quickly as you can.

Flour and sugar make yummy muffins.

Your chore is to rake and pile the leaves.

Sue buys stew and pie for lunch.

CE

Words like friend and believe are hard to spell. We have a little rhyme to help us. We say, "I before E except after C."

Today we are going to read C words, words that are written CE. When C is followed by E (or I or Y) it sounds like an S instead of K. I'm sure you already knew that even if you didn't think about it. Here are some words to read.

ice	rice	mice	nice
spice	twice	prince	mince
space	race	face	lace
France	dance	prance	place
cell	cement	celebrate	celery

Is France a leader in the space race?

Use that spice twice to make the rice.

Let's dance to celebrate!

Pour the cement into place.

Paint the kids' faces like mice.

CI, CY

Here are more words where C sounds like S.

circle   circus   cycle   cyclone
cylinder (sill – in – der)   city

More words:

receive   ceiling   receipt

Do you see what's in the center circle ring at the circus?

Did you receive a receipt from the waiter?

The hot air floats to the ceiling and cools and then falls down again in a cycle.

That's a fancy dance she performed. The lights in the city are bright.

Congratulations! You can read!

PLEASE consider passing this book along to a family in need
by contacting us at allinonehomeschool@gmail.com.

ABOUT THE EASY PEASY ALL-IN-ONE HOMESCHOOL

The Easy Peasy All-in-One Homeschool is a free, complete online homeschool curriculum. There are 180 days of ready-to-go assignments for every level and every subject. It's created for your children to work as independently as you want them to. Preschool through high school is available as well as courses ranging from English, math, science and history to art, music, computer, thinking, physical education and health. A daily Bible lesson is offered as well.

The mission of Easy Peasy is to enable those to homeschool who otherwise thought they couldn't.

Look for other books in the EP Reader Series and for more offline materials to come.

Made in the USA
Columbia, SC
30 April 2017